D1015865

Treasures of Silver

Yea, if thou criest after knowledge, and liftest
up thy voice for understanding; If thou seekest
her as silver, and searchest for her as for hid treasures;
Then shalt thou understand the fear of the Lord,
and find the knowledge of God.

Proverbs 2:3-5

Treasures of Silver

Compiled by

Jo Petty

Published by The C. R. Gibson Company
Norwalk, Connecticut

Contents

The material in this book has
been collected over a long period
of time. Many of the original
sources are unknown to the compiler.
The compiler wishes to acknowledge
the original authors, whoever they
may be, but has confidence that
they would urge, with her, "Do not
inquire as to who said this, but
pay attention to what is said."

*Life without love would be like
the earth without the sun.*

Love

Love is the greatest thing in the world!

> Jesus *loves* the little children
> *All* the children of the world —
> Red and yellow, black and white,
> *All* are precious in His sight.

Every one of us is the object of God's care
as though we were the only one in the world.

God does not play favorites.

> *Jesus loves me, this I know*
> *For the BIBLE tells me so!*

No person is outside the scope of God's love.

When God said 'whosoever', He included me!

God loved us so much that He sent His Son,
Jesus, to earth to show us the way to heaven.

God's love will meet my every need.

> I could talk forever
> Of Jesus' love divine —
> Of all His care and tenderness
> For your life and for mine.

God knows us better than we know ourselves,
and He loves us better, too.

All loves are but a reflection of God's love for us.

I love God because He first loved me.

If I truly love God, I shall love all others.

> To live above with saints we love
> O friend, that will be glory.
> To live below with saints we know
> Is quite a different story.

God loves me in spite of my faults.

I should love others in spite of their faults.

If I love, I love God.

Where love is, there God is.

God is present everywhere and every
person is God's creature.

Hate is like sand in a piece of machinery
and love is like oil.

Hatred is like an acid. It can do more
damage to the vessel in which it is stored
than to the object on which it is poured.

Not where I breathe, but where I love, I live.

Religion is love in action.

Love is the root of all virtues.

Love behaves.

The test of our love for God is the love we
have one for another.

If I love Jesus, I will do what He says.

Heaven and earth shall some day pass away,
but not Jesus' words.

If I love you, I will not lie to you nor
about you.

If I love my parents, I will honor them and
do nothing to make them unhappy.

If I love the poor, I will give to them.

I must even love my enemies.

I must love one who says something bad about me.

If I remember to do Jesus' words, I shall
know the truth and the truth will make me free.

Love is one language everybody understands.

Love doesn't think bad things.

Love does not get angry easily.

Love doesn't brag about me.

Love God and all things will work together for good.

We love when it makes us happier for the other person to be happy than to be happy ourselves.

Love loves to help another.

He who does not love does not know God for God is love.

We owe our love to every person because God made every person and God loves every person.

If I love, that takes care of everything.

Now if I love like this, I know God's love is in me, for my love would not be that loving.

If I love, then I know God lives inside me.

Love praises others.

Love puts up with an awful lot.

Love is funny — the more you give away the more you seem to have left.

Love doesn't get tired.

Love outlasts everything else.

The worst kind of heart trouble is not to
have love in your heart.

Do I love things and use people or love
people and use things?

The most I can do for any person is to love him.

All loves should be stepping-stones to the
love of God.

Work is love you can see.

I must love you like I love myself.

Sometimes it's your turn
and sometimes it's my turn.

Love reminds a friend when he makes a
mistake if he does not seem to know.

Love your enemies, do good to them that hate
you . . . . that you may be children of your Father
which is in heaven: for He makes His sun to
shine on the evil and on the good, and sends
rain on the just and unjust.

Love can't be wasted.

Love never fails!

The only way to have a friend is be one.

A friend is a present you give yourself.

A cheerful friend is like a sunny day.

A true friend is forever a friend.

A friend can seem as close to you as your brother, sometimes closer.

A friend knows all about you — even the bad part — and still loves you.

A friend is one with whom you may dare to be yourself.

You can act any old way with your friend, but you really shouldn't.

Even when I make a fool of myself, my friend still loves me.

Love is patient.

Love is willing to wait.

Love grows.

Love is kind.

Love sees what the eye cannot.

Love hears what the ear cannot.

The heart has reasons that reason does not understand.

> Dear God,
> Help me to do the things I should
> To be to others kind and good,
> In all I do in work or play —
> To grow more loving every day.

Love tells a friend when he gets on the wrong road.

The way I want my friend to treat me is
exactly how I should treat my friend.

Do unto others as though you were the others.

Jesus is my best friend!

Love and you shall be loved.

If nobody loves me, it is my own fault.

The greatest joy is to love and be loved.

He prays best who loves best.

God, Whose Name is Love, will send the best.

We would love each other better if we only understood.

We learn to love better as we grow older.

Love is enough.

Life is nothing but a growing in love.

Not what we receive, but what we give
is the essence of Christian love.

He who sows courtesy reaps friendship,
and he who plants kindness gathers love.

Teach me, Father, when I pray,
Not to ask for more,
But rather let me give my thanks
For what is at my door.
For food and drink, for gentle rain,
For sunny skies above,
For home and friends, for peace and joy,
But most of all for LOVE.

We love ourselves notwithstanding our faults,
and we ought to love our neighbor in a like manner.

We may give without loving,
but we cannot love without giving.

The love of God is broader
Than the measure of man's mind;
And the heart of the Eternal
Is most wonderfully kind.

Love is the law of life.

The language of love is understood by all.

All good gifts around us
Are sent from heaven above;
Then thank the Lord, O thank the Lord
For all His love.

Jesus, what did You find in me
That You have dealt so lovingly?
How great the joy that You have brought
O far exceeding hope or thought.

The end of all learning is to know God,
and out of that knowledge to love and imitate Him.

If our love were but more simple,
We should take Him at His Word,
And our lives would be all sunshine
In the sweetness of the Lord.

How shall I do to love? Believe.
How shall I do to believe? Love.

No door is too difficult for the key of love to open.

God only is the Maker
Of all things near and far:
He paints the wayside flower,
He lights the evening star:
The winds and waves obey Him;
By Him the birds are fed:
Much more to us the children,
He gives our daily bread.

Today, whatever may annoy,
the word for me is JOY, just simple joy.

Joy

Every day is a good day — some are just better than others.

> A Morning Prayer —
> Father, I thank You for the night,
> And for the pleasant morning light,
> For rest and food and loving care,
> And all that makes the day so fair.

Rejoice and be glad today!

> A Morning Song —
> Jesus wants me for a sunbeam
> To shine for Him each day —
> In every way try to please Him,
> At home, at school, at play.

It is more fun to give than to get.

God wants us to be happy.

God made today. I shall be happy today.

God is happy when I pray to Him.

All heaven is happy when I am sorry for my sins and ask God to forgive me.

God has put this joy in my heart.

Do not put off until tomorrow what can be enjoyed today.

The Lord has done great things for us — that's why we are glad.

Joy is everywhere.

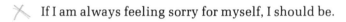 If I am always feeling sorry for myself, I should be.

If I am lonely, it is because I am building walls instead of bridges.

We cannot always control what happens around us, but we can control how we feel about it.

To multiply happiness, divide it.

Not he who has little, but he who wants more is not happy.

To make me happy, do not add to my possessions but subtract from my desires.

Humdrum is not where I live, it is what I am.

Happiness is not getting what you want but
wanting what you get.

I could have things I wish for if I didn't
spend so much time wishing.

Happiness is not where you are going — it is
a manner of traveling.

The secret of being happy is not to do what
you like, but to like what you do.

He who wants little always has enough.

Nobody can take my joy away from me unless I
let them.

God gives me all these beautiful things that
I may enjoy them.

Life is like licking honey off a thorn.

Joy on account of or Joy in spite of?

> When I have thanked the Lord
> For every blessing sent
> But little time will then remain
> For murmur or lament.

We may be sure we are not pleasing God if we
are not happy ourselves.

Few pleasures are more lasting than reading
a good book.

If I learn to forgive others and live with
thanksgiving in my heart and on my lips,
happiness will find me — I will not have to
look for it.

By reading, I can exchange a dull hour for
a happy hour.

I can have more fun at home than any place.

The light that shines the farthest shines
the brightest nearest home.

Joy that isn't shared dies young.

Employ life and you will enjoy life.

Happiness is when we feel close to God.

Sorrow, like rain, makes roses and mud.

When I don't get everything I want, I try to
think of the things I don't get that I don't want.

Wealth is not his that has it, but his that enjoys it.

The main business of life is to enjoy it.

I may be rich and have nothing.

I may be poor and have great riches.

Am I an optimist or a pessimist? Do I call
traffic signals go-lights?

To be wronged is nothing unless I continue
to remember it.

Better to light one candle than to blame the darkness.

I will never injure my eyesight by looking on
the bright side of things.

To speak kindly will not hurt my tongue.

There is no cosmetic for beauty like happiness.

Be cheerful, for of all the things you wear,
the look on your face is the most important.

I am not fully dressed until I put on a smile.

The place to be happy is *here*.

The time to be happy is *now*.

The way to be happy is to help make others happy.

Don't just live and let live, but live and help live.

God loves a cheerful giver.

If you ever find happiness by hunting for it,
you will find it as the old woman did her
lost glasses, safe on her nose all the time.

Happiness is in our own back yard.

All sunshine makes a desert.

The blue of heaven is larger than the clouds.

Defeat isn't bitter if you don't swallow it.

Each new day is a chance to start all over again.

That load becomes light which is cheerfully borne.

Happiness is increased by others but does
not depend on others.

I can be about as happy as I want to be or as sad.

I may be as happy in a cottage as in a mansion.

Pleasant thoughts make pleasant lives.

It takes both rain and sunshine to make a rainbow.

Joy is not in things, it is in us.

Happiness is a thing to be practiced like
a violin.

Manners are the happy way of doing things.

The days that make us happy make us wise.

It is not how much we have, but how much we
enjoy that makes happiness.

Laughter is the outward expression of joy.

I consider my day lost if I have not laughed.

Laughter is the music of the heart.

Joy will escape the narrow confines of the heart.

The happiest person is the one who thinks
the most interesting thoughts and we grow
happier as we grow older.

Duty before pleasure and neither before God.

The best remedy for unhappiness is to count
our blessings.

Do you forget your troubles as easily
as you do your blessings?

If I could count my blessings I would know
the biggest number in the world.

Be thankful for your food and drink.

Thank God for your family and friends.

The Lord daily loads me with benefits.

The morning looks happy. The evening is happy, too.

Praise God from Whom all blessings flow!

I won't confer with sorrow 'til tomorrow.
Today — joy will have her say.

May I not pass this day in search of some
rare and perfect tomorrow.

The cup of life is for him who drinks and
not for him that sips.

Acts of love and kindness never die
But in the lives of others multiply.

Rise and shine!

When you feel dog-tired at night, could it
be because you have growled all day?

If you don't enjoy your own company, why
inflict yourself for hours on somebody else?

Isn't life splendid and isn't it great?
Let's start being happy — it's never too late.

For the beauty of the earth,
For the glory of the skies,
For the love which from our birth
Over and around us lies,
For the wonder of each hour
Of the day and of the night,
Hill and vale, and tree and flower,
Sun and moon, and stars of light,
Lord of all, To Thee we raise
This our hymn of grateful praise.

If I give, it shall be given to me, good
measure, pressed down, and shaken together
and running over.

Sow sparingly, reap sparingly —
Sow bountifully, reap bountifully.

Act as if each day were given you for
Christmas, just as eager, just as proud!

Practice an attitude of gratitude.

A merry heart does good like a medicine.

A merry heart makes a cheerful face.

No joy exceeds the joy of forgiveness.

> Count your joys instead of your woes.
> Count your smiles instead of your tears.
> Count your gains instead of your losses.

Discover the great Indoors !

Today is the only asset I have.

Today is the most important day of my life.

Concentrate on the doughnut instead of the hole.

All the flowers of all the tomorrows are in
the seeds of today.

A good name is rather to be chosen than
great riches, and loving favor rather than
silver and gold.

Let all those that put their trust in God
be happy for God takes care of them.

Serve the Lord with gladness and sing a happy song.

Take joy with you when you go for a walk.

Spilled on the earth are all the joys of heaven.

> I have feet to take me where I'd go,
> I have eyes to see the sunset's glow,
> I have ears to hear what I would hear,
> O God, forgive me when I whine;
> I'm blessed indeed — the world is mine.

Dear Lord, keep us from having our lives so
full of good things that we don't have time
for the best.

No joy exceeds the joy of forgiving and
being forgiven.

> Back of the loaf is the snowy flour,
> And back of the flour the mill:
> And back of the mill is the wheat and the
>   shower,
> And the sun, and the Father's will.

The busy have no time for tears.

If my mind is unemployed, my mind is unenjoyed.

I know what happiness is for I have done good work.

Now I'm not braggin', but it's understood —
What I do, I gotta do good.

The biggest reward for a thing well done is
to have done it.

Every one's work is a self-portrait.

Nobody has more time than I.

Ideas are funny little things. They won't
work unless you do.

I will sing to the Lord for He has been good to me.

> Teach me, my God and King,
> In all things Thee to see;
> And what I do in anything,
> To do it as for Thee.

If I stop to think, I will have reason to thank.

> Be the labor great or small —
> Do it well or not at all.

All people smile in the same language.

> Unlike most things for which we pray,
> A smile we keep when we give it away.

A smile can happen in a flash, but the
memory sometimes lasts forever.

A smile is a curve that can set a lot of
things straight.

Smile for the joy of others.

The best thing to have up your sleeve is
your funny bone.

There is not enough darkness in the whole wide world to put out the light of one little candle.

> Laugh a little — sing a little
> As you go your way!
> Work a little — play a little,
> Do this every day!
>
> Give a little — take a little,
> Never mind a frown —
> Make your smile a welcomed thing
> All around the town!
>
> Laugh a little — love a little,
> Skies are always blue!
> Every cloud has silver linings,
> But it's up to you!

Luck is a very good word if you put a P before it.

Do we enjoy what another needs more?

What word is made shorter by adding a syllable? Answer: Short.

We cannot have mountains without valleys.

The best are not only the happiest, but the happiest are usually the best.

If I try to make others happy, I am happier than they are.

> Sing with gladness
> Banish your sadness!

We can even smile through our tears if we try.

What sunshine is to flowers, smiles are to people.

> Jesus bids us shine,
> With a clear, pure light,
> Like a little candle
> Burning in the night;
> In this world of darkness
> We must shine,
> You in your small corner,
> And I in mine.

You can no more hide the inner feeling of true joy
than you can pour the splendor of the noonday sun
into a mold. Joy will escape the narrow confines
of the human heart.

It isn't our position but our disposition
that makes us happy.

> If you want to be happy,
> Begin where you are,
> Don't wait for some rapture
> That's future and far.
> Begin to be joyous, begin to be glad
> And soon you'll forget
> That you ever were sad.

One thing at a time and that done well
is a very good rule—as many can tell.

Patience

Genius is only patience.

Life is 10% what you make it and 90% how you take it.

There is no failure save in giving up.

We can do most anything we want if we stick to it long enough.

If you never stick your neck out, you'll never get your head above the crowd.

Forget mistakes. Organize victory out of mistakes.

A man can fail many times, but he isn't a failure until he begins to blame somebody else.

The greatest calamity is not to have failed; but to have failed to try.

The only time you mustn't fail is the last
time you try.

Only one person in the whole wide world can
defeat you. That is yourself.

We cannot do everything at once; but we can
do something at once.

A mistake is evidence that someone has tried
to do something.

When the archer misses the center of the
target, he seeks for the cause within himself.

Trying times are times for trying.

Trouble is only opportunity in work clothes.

The difference between stumbling blocks and
stepping-stones is the way we use them.

The secret of patience is doing something
else in the meantime.

Sometimes the best gain is to lose.

Mastery in any art comes only with long practice.

A little more determination, a little more
pluck, a little more work — that's LUCK.

Difficulties strengthen the mind, as labor
does the body.

I will not fail unless I give up trying.

Failing is not falling, but in failing to
rise when you fall.

You may if you try —
You won't if you don't.

If at first you don't succeed, you are
running about average.

The burdens don't matter as long as I remember to give them to God.

No difficulties, no discovery.
No pains, no gain.

The more difficult the obstacle, the
stronger one becomes after hurdling it.

The secret of success is hard work.

Education is hard, hard work, but it can be
made interesting work.

The grass may seem greener on the other side,
but it is just as hard to mow.

A smooth sea never made a skillful mariner.

The dictionary is the only place where success
comes before work.

The quitter never wins.

The winner never quits.

You can't slide uphill.

An ounce of pluck is worth a ton of luck.

If at first you do succeed, try something harder.

Experience is what makes you wonder how it got a reputation for being the best teacher.

When you begin to coast you know you are on the downgrade.

It does one good to be somewhat parched by the heat and drenched by the rain of life.

To find fault is easy; to do better may be difficult.

Shoot at everything and hit nothing.

Make haste slowly.

Pure gold can lie for a month in the furnace without losing a grain.

It isn't the mountain ahead that wears you out — it's the grain of sand in your shoe.

Instead of waiting upon the Lord, some people want the Lord to wait upon them.

Every time you give another a "piece of your mind", you add to your own vacuum.

The night is not forever.

Itching for what you want doesn't do much
good; you've got to scratch for it.

If all men are created equal, it is because
they have 24 hours a day.

It is easier to be critical than correct.

Firmness is that admirable quality in ourselves that is merely stubbornness in others.

Pay to no one evil for evil.

Be not weary in well doing.

Overcome evil with good.

Be patient with everyone.

Murmur not.

If you can't have the best of everything,
make the best of everything you have.

The man who rows the boat doesn't have time
to rock it.

Do the truth you know and you shall learn
the truth you need to know.

Before you flare up at any one's faults,
take time to count ten — ten of your own.

There's no sense in advertising your troubles.
There is no market for them.

Telling your troubles always helps. The
world's dumb indifference makes you mad
enough to keep on trying.

Why value the present hour less than some
future hour?

If you don't scale the mountain, you can't
see the view.

It isn't the load that weighs us down — it's
the way we carry it.

> Let us then, be up and doing
> With a heart for any fate,
> Still achieving, still pursuing,
> Learn to labor and to wait.

When you think you are at the end of your
rope, tie a knot in it and hang on!

The late blooming virtues can be the very best.

If we hope for that we see not, then do we
with patience wait for it.

> Life is hard by the yard —
> By the inch, it's cinch.

When God makes an oak tree, he takes 20 years.
He takes only two months to make a squash.

The diamond cannot be polished without
friction, nor man perfected without trials.

The aim of education is to teach us how to
think, not what to think.

Instruction may end in the schoolroom, but
education ends only with life.

Character development is the true aim of education.

One learns manners from those who have none.

Were I chaste as ice and pure as snow, I
should not escape slander.

You are only young once, but you can stay
immature almost indefinitely.

When you are through changing, you're through.

Age has many blessings youth cannot understand.

Will Power! Won't Power! Supreme Power!

Habit is a cable; we weave a thread of it
every day; and at last we cannot break it.

We first make our habits, and then our habits make us.

The chains of habit are generally too small
to be felt until they are too strong to be broken.

Habit, if not resisted, soon becomes necessity.

Everything comes to him who waits, if he
works while he waits.

> One thing at a time and that done well
> Is a very good rule — as many can tell.

Housework is something you do that nobody
notices unless you don't do it.

God never makes us conscious of our weakness
except to give us of His strength.

Anytime a person takes a stand, there'll
come a time when he'll be tested to see how
firm his feet are planted.

Poise is the art of raising the eyebrows
instead of the roof.

Don't lessen the lesson.

He surely is most in need of another's
patience who has none of his own.

No one is as old as he hopes to be.

No wise man ever wished to be younger.

A stitch in time saves nine.

Better to slip with the foot than with the tongue.

Better let them wonder why you didn't talk
than why you did.

Habits are first cobwebs, then cables.

Commit a sin twice, and it will seem no longer a sin.

Habit can be my best friend or my worst enemy.

A loose tongue often gets into a tight place.

Is it true? Is it necessary? Will it help?

Use speech for spreading good will.

He who keeps his mouth and his tongue keeps
his soul from troubles.

He that can rule his tongue shall live
without strife.

A fool utters all his mind; but a wise man
keeps it in till afterwards.

It's all right to hold a conversation, but
you should let go of it now and then.

Even a fool, when he holds his peace, is counted wise.

He that has knowledge spares his words.

He that refrains his lips is wise.

In a multitude of words there lacks not sin.

I shall give account on the day of judgment
for every idle word I speak.

I have often regretted my speech, seldom my silence.

Tact is the ability to close your mouth
before someone else wants to.

Think all you speak, but speak not all you think.

Nothing is opened more by mistake than the mouth.

Best rule I know for talking is the same as
the one for carpentering — Measure twice and
saw once.

Brevity is the soul of wit and even wit is
a burden when it talks too long.

They think too little who talk too much.

Some people need a double chin. There's too
much work for one.

We weaken what we exaggerate.

Listening is wanting to hear.

A good listener is not only popular everywhere, but after a while he knows something.

Tact is the unsaid part of what you think.

Words in haste do friendships waste.

'A soft answer turns away wrath' is the best
system of self-defense.

Who gossips to you will gossip of you.

When music speaks, all other voices should cease.

Taste your words before you let them pass your teeth.

Do not say a little in many words, but a
great deal in a few.

The longer you keep your temper, the more
it will improve.

Silence is not always golden — sometimes it
is just plain yellow.

Prayer:
Set a watch, O Lord, before my mouth; keep
the door of my lips. Let me say the right
things rightly.

Temper, if ungoverned, governs the whole person.

When angry count ten before you speak; if
very angry, count a hundred.

Let not the sun go down upon your wrath.

He who can suppress a moment's anger may
prevent a day of sorrow.

Swallowing your pride occasionally will
never give you indigestion.

A small leak will sink a great ship.

People who fly into a rage always make a
bad landing.

There are times when nothing a man can say
is nearly so powerful as saying nothing.

It is easy to dodge an elephant but not a fly.

The gilding of the key will not make it open
the door better.

Your body is for use — not abuse.

Dope is for dopes.

Think: Will this turn me on or will it turn on me?

Work is the best narcotic.

The key to a lot of troubles is the one that
fits the ignition.

Statistics prove folk who drive like crazy are.

The first step in making a dream come true
is to wake up.

A college graduate is a person who had a
chance to get an education.

As easy as falling off a diet.

Will power is the ability to eat
one salted peanut.

The archer who overshoots his mark does no better than he who falls short of it.

Do you act or react?

There's a slight difference between keeping your chin up and sticking your neck out, but it's worth knowing.

Taste makes waist.

Laziness travels so slowly that poverty soon overtakes him.

Thrift is a wonderful virtue — especially in ancestors.

Spend less than you get.

A penny saved is as good as a penny earned.

Waste not, want not.

Willful waste makes woeful want.

Stretching the truth won't make it last any longer.

If I know enough to do a thing, I know enough not to do a thing.

Don't tell your friends about your indigestion: 'How are you' is a greeting, not a question.

Prejudice is being down on what we are not up on.

If you blame others for your failures, do
you credit others with your successes?

Old-timers who recall the hip-deep snows of
their childhood should remember that when
they were children their hips were lower.

To sin by silence when they should protest,
makes cowards of men.

If you have a weakness, make it work for
you as a strength — and if you have a
strength, don't abuse it into a weakness.

Somebody thought Anybody would do it, and
Somebody thought Everybody should.
Guess who finally did it?
That's right — Nobody.

Everybody's business is nobody's business.

Wouldn't it be nice if we could find other
things as easily as we find fault?

God has a song to teach us, and when we have
learned it amid the shadows of affliction,
we can sing it forever.

> Good timber does not grow in ease,
> The stronger wind, the stronger trees;
> The farther sky, the greater length,
> The more the storms, the more the strength.
> By sun and cold, by rain and snow,
> In tree or man good timber grows.

A man shows what he is by what he does with what he has.

Many of the things that go wrong surprise us
by turning out all right.

More people would be on Easy Street if they
were willing to go through a tough neighborhood
to get there.

The greatest and sublimest power is often simple patience.

The cloud that darkens the present hour may brighten
all our future days.

Free enterprise gives everybody a chance to get to
the top. Some depend on the free and not enough on
the enterprise.

An ounce of pluck is worth a ton of luck.

> Not so in haste, my heart,
> Have faith in God and wait:
> Although He lingers very long,
> He never comes too late.

> God never comes too late,
> He knows what is best.
> Vex not thyself today in vain,
> Until He comes, I rest.

Dear Lord, Help me never to judge another until I have walked two weeks in his shoes.

Meekness

God has two dwellings: one in heaven and
the other in a meek and thankful heart.

Meekness is surrendering to God.

A child may have more real wisdom than a
brilliant philosopher who does not know God.

Though the Lord be high, He has respect unto
the lowly.

If I exalt myself, I shall be abased, if I
humble myself, I shall be exalted.

Humble yourself under the mighty Hand of God
and He will exalt you in due time.

God resists the proud, but gives grace to the humble.

When I think I stand, I should take heed
lest I fall!

Before honor is humility.

They that know God will be humble; they that
know themselves cannot be proud.

Humility is a strange thing. The minute you
think you've got it, you've lost it.

Learn from the mistakes of others — you can't
live long enough to make them all yourself.

True greatness consists in being great in
little things.

> What if the little rain should say,
> "As small a drop as I
> Can never refresh a drooping earth,
> I'll tarry in the sky."

Nothing is too small to play a part in God's scheme.

It is they who do their duties in every-day
and trivial matters who also fulfill them on
great occasions.

Everyone is ignorant — only on different subjects.

God's strength is made perfect in weakness.

An admission of error is a sign of strength
rather than a confession of weakness.

When success turns a man's head, he is fac-
ing failure.

To err may be human, but to admit it isn't.

I'd admit my faults, if I had any.

It is better to understand a little than to misunderstand a lot.

We may be taught by every person we meet.

A man wrapped up in himself makes a very small bundle.

The more you know, the more you know you don't know.

Most people's hindsight is 20/20.

It is no advantage for a man to know much unless he lives according to what he knows.

Nothing is done finally and right.

Nothing is known positively and completely.

A wise son makes a glad father.

Children should hear the instruction of their parents.

The ways of man are before the eyes of the Lord, and He ponders all his goings.

Receive with meekness the engrafted Word which is able to save your soul.

God gives grace to the lowly.

A meek and quiet spirit is of great price
in the sight of God.

Jesus came not to be ministered unto, but
to minister, and to give His life a ransom
for many.

In honor prefer one another.

Submit yourself to every ordinance of man
for the Lord's sake for so is the will of God.

If anyone asks you to go a mile, go with him two.

I am only one, but I am one. I cannot do
everything, but I can do something.

> Are you sure that you are Right?
> How fine and strong!
> But were you ever just as sure —
> And wrong?

The greatest truths are the simplest and so
are the greatest men.

The common people heard Jesus gladly.

A man's life does not consist in the abund-
ance of things which he possesses.

I brought nothing into this world, and it is
certain I shall carry nothing out.

I am the clay, and God is the potter; and I
am the work of His Hand!

Whosoever shall keep the commandments and
teach them, he shall be called great in the
kingdom of heaven.

Man shall not live by bread alone, but by
every word that proceeds out of the mouth of God.

Let not the rich man glory in his riches.

Glory only in the Lord.

Every one of us shall give account of himself
to God. Let us not therefore judge one another.

Dear Lord, Help me never to judge another
until I have walked two weeks in his shoes.

God understands my thoughts afar off and is
acquainted with all my ways. There is not a
word in my tongue, but He knows it.

Boast not yourself of tomorrow; for you
know not what a day may bring forth.

I should say, if the Lord will, I shall live,
and do this or that, for I know not what
shall be on the morrow.

The Lord is near unto them that are of a
broken heart; and saves such as be of a
contrite spirit.

The Lord can mend my broken heart if I give
Him *all* the pieces.

Love not the praise of men more than the
praise of God.

Let another man praise me and not my own
mouth; a stranger and not my own lips.

Dear Lord, Let the words of my mouth and
the meditation of my heart be pleasing in Your sight.

Let not the wise man glory in his wisdom.

There is more hope for a fool than for a
man wise in his own conceits.

I am not conceited, though I do have every
reason to be.

God has chosen the foolish things of the
world to confound the wise.

Let not the mighty man glory in his might.

God has chosen the weak things of the world
to confound the mighty.

A mighty man is not delivered by much strength.

> The dewdrop, as the boundless sea
> In God's great plan has part;
> And this is all He asks of thee,
> Be faithful, where thou art.

Meekness is not weakness.

Humility is a kind of gratitude.

Let the little children come unto Jesus:
for of such is the kingdom of heaven!

Kindness is a language the dumb can speak
and the deaf understand.

I can be kind in looks, words and acts.

Every deed of love and kindness done to man
is done to God.

One cannot find any rule of conduct to excel
'simplicity' and 'sincerity'.

True nobility comes of the gentle heart.

A gentleman is a gentle man.

Be kind one to another, tenderhearted, forgiving one another even as God for Christ's
sake has forgiven you.

Nothing will make us so kind and tender to the faults
of others as to thoroughly examine ourselves.

Be kind, for everyone you meet is fighting a
hard battle.

Rejoice with them that do rejoice and weep
with them that weep.

The merciful shall obtain mercy.

He that has mercy on the poor, happy is he.

A candle-glow can pierce the darkest night.

Do you care for the poor at your door?

Be gentle to all people.

We cannot always oblige, but we can always
speak obligingly.

The Lord is good and ready to forgive; and
plenteous in mercy unto all them who call upon Him.

> I have wept in the night for the shortness
>   of sight
> That to somebody's need made me blind;
> But I never have yet felt a twinge of regret
> For being a little too kind.

The kindly word that falls today may bear
its fruit tomorrow.

The art of being kind is all this world needs.

When we forgive ourselves and others, God
will forgive us.

A non-forgiving heart cannot be forgiven.

Forgiveness is the sweet smell the violet
sheds on the heel that crushed it.

Nothing is so strong as gentleness and
nothing so gentle as real strength.

The more perfect we are, the more gentle and
quiet we become toward the defects of others.

The test of good manners is being able to put
up pleasantly with bad ones.

> Be to his virtues very kind —
> Be to his faults a little blind.

Disagree without being disagreeable.

Punctuality is the politeness of kings and the
duty of gentle people everywhere.

True politeness is perfect ease and freedom;
it simply consists in treating others as you
love to be treated yourself.

A small unkindness is a great offense.

Jesus said that seven times is not enough to forgive.
He said forgive seventy times seven times.

Love ever gives and forgives.

Few things are more bitter than to feel bitter.

Talk to God as friend to friend.

It takes two to quarrel and it takes two to
make up after a quarrel.

I really should be first to say hello — first
to smile — and, if necessary, first to forgive.

If I am stronger than another, I should do
more for him than he does for me.

A good memory is fine — but the ability to
forget is the true test of greatness.

Has someone drawn a circle and shut you out?
You and Love can outsmart him. Draw a bigger
circle and take him in.

It is right that we remember wrongs done to
us so that we may forgive those who wronged
us.

It is in pardoning others that God pardons us.

If you are not for yourself, who will be for you?

If you are for yourself alone, then why are you?

Listening is a way of loving.

> I was angry with my friend,
> I told my wrath, my wrath did end.
> I was angry with my foe;
> I hid my wrath, my wrath did grow.

Maturity is humility. A mature person is able to say,
"I was wrong." He is also able to say, "I am sorry."
And when he is proven right, he does not have to say,
"I told you so."

A smart alec is a person who thinks he knows
as much as I know I do.

Education is the process whereby one goes from
cocksure ignorance to thoughtful uncertainty.

> Little drops of water,
> Little grains of sand,
> Make the mighty ocean
> And the pleasant land.

> And the little moments,
> Humble though they be,
> Make the mighty ages
> Of eternity.

Don't brag — it isn't the whistle that pulls the train.

> A humble, lowly, contrite heart,
> Believing, true, and clean,
> Which neither life nor death can part
> From Him who dwells within.

Be not like the cock who thought the sun rose
to hear him crow.

Meekness is that temper of spirit in which we
accept God's dealing with us as good.

I can see my true significance only after I have
realized my insignificance.

There is no surer sign of perfection than a
willingness to be corrected.

The smallest good deed is better than the grandest good intention.

Goodness

To every one there opens a high way and a
  low —
And each person decides the way his soul
  shall go!

No one has a right to do as he pleases,
except when he pleases to do right.

If you do what you should not, you must bear
what you would not.

Whatever I sow, that I shall reap.

All things whatsoever I would that others
should do to me, I must do even so to them.

The EYES of the Lord are in every place
beholding the evil and the good.

Even a child is known by his doings, whether
his work be pure, and whether it be right.

Goodness

Do I practice the behavior I expect from others?

Sow an act and you reap a habit.
Sow a habit and you reap a character.
Sow a character and you reap a destiny.

If you want to put the world right, start with yourself.

He who reforms himself has done much toward
reforming others.

> If the whole world followed you,
> Followed to the letter,
> Tell me — if it followed you,
> Would the world be better?

Let us seek not to be better than our neighbors,
but better than ourselves.

> Prayer:
> Jesus, Friend of little children,
> Be a friend to me;
> Take my hand and ever keep me
> Close to Thee.
> Teach me how to grow in goodness
> Daily as I grow;
> You have been a child,
> And surely You must know.

Life is not the wick or the candle — it is
the burning.

A man is rich according to what he is, not
according to what he has.

Be what you wish others to become.

Resolve to be better for the echo of it.

If anyone speaks evil of you, so live that none will believe it.

Reputation is what people think we are. Character is what God knows we are.

The only way to settle a disagreement is on the basis of what's right — not who's right.

There is no right way to do the wrong thing.

We've got to build a better man before we build a better world.

One sinner destroys much good.

If you are not able to make yourself what you wish, how can you expect to mould another to your will?

If I were faultless I would not be so much annoyed by the defects of others.

The Devil has many tools, but a lie is the handle that fits them all.

You are not better for being praised nor worse for being blamed.

Doing right is no guarantee against misfortune.

Always tell the truth and you won't need a good memory.

Spend so much time on the improvement of yourself
that you have no time to criticize others.

Do right and leave the results with God.

Liberty is not the right to do as we please,
but the opportunity to do what is right.

The earth is full of the goodness of the Lord.

> All things bright and beautiful,
> All creatures great and small;
> All things wise and wonderful,
> The Lord God made them all.
>
> Each little flower that opens,
> Each little bird that sings,
> He made their glowing colors,
> He made their tiny wings.
>
> He gave us eyes to see them,
> And lips that we might tell
> How good is God our Father,
> Who does all things well.

God is faithful. While the earth remains,
seedtime and harvest, cold and heat, and
summer and winter, and day and night shall
not cease.

God is good and He loves us always and in all ways.

Be quiet and think on God's goodness.

Cast out the beam from your own eye; and you
shall see clearly to cast the mote out of
your brother's eye.

Create in me a clean heart, O.God; and renew
a right spirit within me, I pray.

Let us bear one another's burdens, and so
fulfil the law of Christ.

Feed the hungry, give drink to the thirsty,
take into your home the strangers, clothe
the naked, visit the sick and those in
prison. Inasmuch as we do these things unto
the least of our brothers, we do them unto
Jesus.

Speak not evil one of another.

Ever follow that which is good to all men.

Render not evil for evil unto any person.

Be a doer of the word, and not a hearer only,
deceiving your own self.

Don't mistake potatoes for principles or peas for piety.

You are not what you think you are, but you
are what you think.

We see things not as they are, but as we are.

The greatest of faults is to be conscious of none.

Sin is the transgression of the law.

Fools make a mock at sin.

My sins have withheld good things from me.

He who covers his sins shall not prosper:
but whoso confesses and forsakes them shall
have mercy.

We don't break God's laws — we break ourselves on them.

Are you trying to make something for yourself or something of yourself?

A lie has no legs. It requires other lies
to support it. Tell one lie and you are
forced to tell others to back it up.

Conscience is the still small voice that
makes you feel still smaller.

Abstain from all appearance of evil.

Honest gain is the only permanent gain.

> For when the One great Scorer comes,
> To write against your name,
> He writes not that you lost or won
> But how you played the game.

To be good is fine, but to be proud of it
ruins the whole thing.

A criminal is nothing else but you and me at
our weakest, found out.

Discover what is true and practice what is good.

Many faults in our neighbor should be of
less concern to us than one of the smallest
in ourselves.

Would you like to see the most dangerous
animal in the world — the one that can harm
you the most? Look in the mirror.

The hand that's dirty with honest labor is
fit to shake with any neighbor.

As we have opportunity, let us do good unto all men.

No one can be good to others without being
good to himself.

To him that knows to do good, and does it
not, to him it is a sin.

I am asking when I pray 'Our Father' to live
here as it is done there.

Pretty is as pretty does.

It shall be well with the righteous: for
they shall eat the fruit of their doing.

It shall be ill to the wicked: for the
reward of his hands shall be given him.

If I am faithful in that which is least, I
shall be faithful also in much.

If I am unjust in the least, I shall be unjust also in much.

To whom much is given, of him much shall be required.

Prove all things; hold fast that which is good.

Lying lips are abomination to the Lord; but
they that deal truly are His delight.

Be holy in all manner of conversation.

The pure in heart shall see God.

If I say I abide in Jesus, I should walk as He walked.

If you talk the talk, baby, walk the walk.

I shall to my own self be true. If I am true to
those around me, I shall be true to myself.

The man who trims himself to suit everybody
will soon whittle himself away.

What you dislike in another, take care to
correct in yourself.

Only the best behavior is good enough for
daily use in the home.

Do the best things in the worst times.

Nobody's perfect, but I'm close.

Can my creed be recognized in my deed?

Man looks on the outward appearance; but God
looks on the heart.

Sin is not in things, but in the wrong use of things.

Be what you say and say what you are.

Honesty is always the best policy.

A problem honestly stated is half solved.

Truth cannot be killed with the sword or
gun nor abolished by law.

It is easy to tell a lie; but hard to tell only one lie.

It is better to suffer for speaking the truth than
that the truth should suffer for want of speaking it.

Prefer loss before unjust gain.

Oh, what a tangled web we weave, when first
we practice to deceive.

If I am not liberal with what I have, I
deceive myself if I think I would be more
liberal if I had more.

If I wish to secure the good of others, I
have already secured my own.

Keep your nose clean so you can smell a phoney.

If the cake is bad, what good is the icing.

From the errors of others a wise man corrects his own.

The prodigal robs his heir; the miser robs himself.

Talent may develop in solitude, but character is developed in society.

The man who lives by himself and for himself is apt to be corrupted by the company he keeps.

Progress is not changing, but changing for the better.

Your luck is how you treat people.

I am the temple of God, and the Spirit of God dwells in me. I must not defile the temple.

The Spirit Itself bears witness with my spirit, that I am a child of God.

He who lives to live forever never fears dying.

Live virtuously and you cannot die too soon nor live too long.

Life is a journey, not a home.

What I am to be, I am now becoming.

My part is to improve the present moment.

It takes the whole of life to learn how to live.

Ever follow that which is good to all men.

Blessings are upon the head of the just.

> Every virtue we possess;
> And every victory won;
> And every thought of holiness,
> Are God's alone.

Help your brother's boat across, and lo!
your own has reached the shore.

Is there anything in the world more spacious
than the room we have for improvement?

> Breathe on me, Breath of God,
> Fill me with life anew,
> That I may love what thou dost love,
> And do what thou wouldst do.

*If we do not find peace in ourselves,
it is vain to seek it elsewhere.*

Inner Peace

Peace is the happy, natural state of a person.

To carry care to bed is to sleep with a
pack on your back.

The peace within becomes the harmony without.

> Worry never climbed a hill
> Worry never paid a bill
> Worry never dried a tear
> Worry never calmed a fear
> Worry never darned a heel
> Worry never cooked a meal
> Worry never led a horse to water
> Worry never done a thing you'd think it
>   oughta.

Worry — a mental tornado — a dog chasing
its own tail.

Anger is a wind which blows out the lamp of the mind.

The fella who worries about what people
think of him wouldn't worry so much if he
only knew how little they do.

I do my best and leave the outcome to God.

With God, go even over the sea;
Without Him, not over the threshold.

Jesus prays for me!

The Holy Spirit prays for me!

God sees farther than I do.

Think little of what others think of you.

> There is no place to hide a sin,
> Without the conscience looking in!

Be sure your sins will find you out.

Fear nothing so much as sin.

There is no peace, says the Lord, unto the wicked.

No pleasure can quiet my conscience.

Money can't buy a clean conscience — square
dealing is the price tag.

Jesus Christ the same yesterday, today and forever!!!!

Faith is as sure as the sight of the sun.

Faith is as sure as the feel of a loving touch.

It's right to be content with what you have,
but never with what you are.

The light that shows us our sin is the light
that heals us.

A clean conscience is a soft pillow.

As long as I stand in my own way, everything
seems to be in my way.

When you have finished your day, go to sleep
in peace; God is awake!

I will lay me down in peace and sleep for
Thou, Lord, only makes me dwell in safety.

Cast all your care upon God, for He cares for you.

No one is safe who does not learn to trust
God for every thing.

Any trouble that is too small to take to
God in prayer is too small to worry about.

In times when I am afraid, I will trust in God.

God comforts me like my mother comforts me.

Faith is as sure as the sound of thunder.

A tiny seed can fill a field with flowers.

Faith is the victory that overcomes.

Be still, and know that I am God.

When I am still, I know that I am His.

God is only a prayer away.

Draw near to God and He will draw near to you.

Take one step toward God and
He will take two steps toward you.

Prayer changes things. Prayer changed me!

God shall supply all my need according to His
riches in glory by Christ Jesus.

God will supply, but we must apply.

> Closer is God than breathing —
> Nearer than hands or feet.

We cannot go where God is not.

Freely God has promised, boldly I may ask.

To be a seeker is soon to be a finder.

Faith is a gift of God.

We get faith by hearing God's Word.

I cannot have a need Jesus cannot supply.

God sends His angels to keep me from harm.

Faith is as certain as the existence of water.

God's eye is on the sparrow, and I know He watches me.

Though we travel the world over to find the
beautiful, we must carry it with us or we find it not.

One who is afraid of lying is usually afraid
of nothing else.

Fear God and all other fears will disappear.

In the great quiet of God my troubles are
but the pebbles on the road. My joys are
the everlasting hills.

Faith is as sure as the taste of an apple.

Faith is as sure as the fragrance of a rose.

God gives the very best to those who leave
the choice with Him.

The law of prayer is more powerful and just
as universal as the law of gravity.

How calmly may we trust ourselves to the
Hands of Him Who bears up the world.

God holds everybody in His Hands!

Faith stands leaning on God's Word.

Faith expects nothing from ourselves and
everything from God.

Ask, and it shall be given me; seek, and I
shall find; knock, and it shall be opened unto me.

With God all things are possible.

God is able to do much more than we can ask or think.

As the heavens are higher than the earth, so
are God's ways higher than my ways and God's
thoughts are higher than my thoughts.

We pray "God's will be done".

If God be for me, who can be against me?

I know not what the future holds, but I know
Who holds the future.

My help comes from the Lord, Who made heaven
and earth.

> Jesus came to die on a cross of wood
> Yet made the hill on which it stood.

God has made the earth, and created man
upon it. His Hand stretched out the heavens,
and all their host has He commanded.

Our strength lies in our dependence upon God.

Because I have faith I understand that the
worlds were framed by the Word of God and
that things which I see were not made of
things which I see.

God said, "Let there be Light" and there was Light!

In Christ are hid all the treasures of
wisdom and knowledge.

I am a child of God by faith in Christ Jesus.

In God I live, and move, and have my being.

I can only deny God with the breath He gives me.

There is an outward me and there is an
inward me.

Though the outward me will someday perish,
the inward me is renewed day by day.

My body is only my house — it is not the
really, really me. That's why I can be
happy no matter what.

> Said the robin to the sparrow,
> "I should really like to know
> Why these anxious human beings
> Rush around and worry so."
> Said the sparrow to the robin,
> "Friend, I think that it must be
> That they have no Heavenly Father
> Such as cares for you and me."

As my day so shall my strength be.

I can do all things through Christ Who strengthens me.

Do not worry about whether the sun will
rise; be prepared to enjoy it.

Take no thought for food or drink or clothes
for your heavenly Father knows you have need
of these things.

Seek God first and all these things shall be
added unto you.

If I seek the Lord, I shall not want any
good thing.

If I trust in the Lord and do good, I shall
have a place to live and I shall be fed.

Trust God in every way every day.

Faith takes God at His word whatever He says.

Continue in prayer and give thanks.

Good prayer says 'please' and 'thank you' at
the same time.

God listens to our hearts rather than to our lips.

A little boy knelt to pray. He said his
ABC's but told his mother God could take
the letters and form them into words.

When you pray, don't say, "hello God" and
hang up the receiver. Wait for God to answer. Listen.

Pray for others.

You cannot pray the Lord's Prayer and even
once say I — From the very beginning it never
once says me.
Our Father — Give us — Lead us — Deliver us —

A tea party is no fun if there is no one
there but me, myself, and I.

Whatever we beg of God, let us also work for it.

Pray our work and work our prayers.

Pray to God for potatoes but remember the hoe.

God is the source of all I need or all I
could ever want.

Everything I do is a miracle.

The Lord is my shepherd; I shall not want.

Goodness and mercy shall follow me all the
days of life; and I will dwell in the
house of the Lord forever.

Whatever God sends, whether sunshine or
rain, it is needed for that inner me's health.

The ole Devil trembles when he sees me upon my knees.

I love the Lord and all things will work
together for good to me.

I walk by faith, not by sight.

All I see teaches me to trust the Creator
for all I do not see.

If I can see the Invisible, I can do the impossible.

With God, nothing shall be impossible.

One (and I am one) on God's side is a majority.

No real peace can abide with the man who lives
contrary to the Word of God. In all the storms that
beat upon the soul, one who stands on the promises
of God has stability and calm. In the keeping of
God's commandments there are great rewards and peace
is only one of them.

To be spiritually minded is life and peace.

> Only be still and wait God's leisure
> In cheerful hope, with heart content
> To take whatever your Father's pleasure,
> Knowing it is what Love has sent.

In all your ways acknowledge God, and He shall
direct your paths.

With Christ as my Savior, I need neither fear the
present nor be apprehensive of the future. I am
safe and secure in His hands.

God is our refuge and strength, a very present help
in trouble. Therefore will not we fear, though the
earth be removed, and though the mountains be
carried into the midst of the sea.

When you can't sleep, do you count sheep?
No, I talk with the Shepherd.

> In heavenly love abiding,
> No change my heart shall fear,
> And safe is such confiding,
> For nothing changes here.
> The storm may roar without me,
> My heart may low be laid;
> But God is round about me,
> And can I be dismayed?

The secret of contentment is know how to enjoy what
you have.

The load of tomorrow added to that of yesterday
carried today makes the strongest falter.

No time is lost waiting upon the Lord.

> O bless the Lord, my soul!
> His mercies bear in mind!
> Forget not all his benefits!
> The Lord to thee is kind.

The prayer of the upright is God's delight.

Faith is not belief without proof, but trust without
reservations.

A grudge is too heavy a load for anyone to bear.

Prayer is so simple. It is like quietly opening a
door and stepping into the very presence of God.

It is not the greatness of my faith that moves
mountains, but my faith in the greatness of God.

You are not a reservoir with a limited amount of
resources: you are a channel attached to unlimited
divine resources.

Never think that God's delays are God's denials.

Every good gift and every perfect gift is from above,
and cometh down from the Father of lights, with whom
is no variableness, neither shadow of turning.

Do the very best you can and leave the outcome to God.

> The King of love my shepherd is,
> Whose goodness faileth never;
> I nothing lack if I am his,
> And he is mine forever.

He does not say, 'at the end of the way you find Me.'
He says, 'I AM the way: I AM the road under your feet,
the road that begins just as low as you happen to be.'

O Lord, may I practice what I preach, and preach what
I practice.

Blessed are the peacemakers: for they shall be called
the children of God.

The Lord is my light and my salvation; whom shall I
fear? the Lord is the strength of my life; of whom
shall I be afraid?

Fear God and all other fears will disappear.

Peace I leave with you, my peace I give unto you: not
as the world giveth, give I unto you. Let not your
heart be troubled, neither let it be afraid.

Be careful for nothing; but in every thing by prayer
and supplication with thanksgiving let your requests
be made known unto God. And the peace of God, which
passeth all understanding, shall keep your hearts and
minds through Christ Jesus.

> Wherever he may guide me,
> No want shall turn me back;
> My Shepherd is beside me,
> And nothing can I lack.
> His wisdom ever waketh,
> His sight is never dim.
> He knows the way he taketh,
> And I will walk with him.

Sow a Thought and you reap an Act;
Sow an Act and you reap a Habit;
Sow a Habit and you reap a Character;
Sow a Character and you reap a Destiny.

Set in Melior, roman and italic,
a typeface designed by Herman Zapf.

Designed by Gordon Brown